A SOLDIER'S FORTUNE

AND OTHER  POEMS

ED BROWN

Agio
PUBLISHING HOUSE

PUBLISHING HOUSE

151 Howe Street, Victoria BC Canada V8V 4K5

www.agiopublishing.com

A Soldier's Fortune and Other Poems
ISBN 978-1-927755-04-4 (trade paperback)
ISBN 978-1-927755-05-1 (ebook)

Cataloguing information available from
Library and Archives Canada.
Printed on acid-free paper.
Agio Publishing House is a socially responsible company,
measuring success on a triple-bottom-line basis.
10 9 8 7 6 5 4 3 2 1a

POET'S NOTE & DEDICATION

When I started writing poems I did it with three thoughts in mind:
- First was to get the crap out of my head so I could better understand it and help myself process and heal.
- Second, I wanted other people to understand how combat and peacekeeping affects us and our families. I will never understand what it's like to have a parent or spouse come home a different person because I was the one who was changed. I can only verbalize that I myself went though emotional hell trying to understand. I endured physical injuries as well as emotional. Would I do it again to serve my country? Hell, yeah.
- My third thought: If I could give strength to another as some have done for me. If the burden of pain is shared then it becomes less painful.

I would like to dedicate this book to my parents and my children who gave me strength when I needed it most. To my family and friends who have supported me and were there when I needed to chat. To my beautiful gal who loves me as I am. I love you all.

I would like to thank the counsellors and doctors who help patch us up. I am a better man today because of help from my health professionals and the Military Family Resource Centre staff.

A final dedication to those who serve and the families that support them.

TABLE OF CONTENTS

WAR OF THE MIND

A SOLDIER'S FORTUNE

A soldier's fortune of coming home
To a wife that does not recognize you
Your mind not your own.

A soldier's fortune as death draws so near
Bullets flying right past your ear.
A soldier's fortune of serving a cause
So much death I ponder and pause.

A soldier's fortune of a spirit broke.
A soldier's fortune of atrocities spoke.

A job that he loves is taken away
Unable to trust you with a rifle they say.

Family broken.
No one can say. Just why Daddy came back that way.

A soldier's fortune so proud to serve
Then they take it away
No longer can he fight
The fucking nerve.

I came back from my last tour and had some problems dealing with things. My doctor told me that I would not see another tour again. This was extremely hard to hear. Not only was I very angry toward my family and life in general but being told that you can no longer serve your country is hard for a soldier to hear. I loved to serve and was very proud. I felt that had been ripped away from me. This caused me to become even more bitter and angry. It was an extremely hard transition for me to make.

We as soldiers are so proud to serve. I was a career soldier. I would have stayed in the military until I was ready to retire. But all things happen for a reason. We just don't always recognize it at the time.

DEMONS HIDE

Demons hide
In my mind
Twist my soul
I'm not whole
My spirit wrought
My body broke
Kill me now
My life a joke
In my mind
You will see
Demons fire
Burning me
Hiding behind
Eyes so cold
Demons hide
So fucking bold
Save me now
Set me free
From demons hiding
And haunting me
As I close my eyes
And try to sleep
God I beg
From demons keep.

Some vets return from overseas having vivid and violent thoughts running through their head. For a mild mannered person this can be quite troublesome. There were times I felt I was haunted by a demon, corrupting my dreams and twisting my thoughts. I had bouts of hatred and anger that I did not understand. If it were not for being able to speak openly to my psychologist and psychiatrist from the Base I feel I would have gone nuts. I felt so much shame for these feelings I did not understand. I experienced even more shame for feeling that I had let my family down and was causing them so much grief and pain.

I am so glad that I had great people in my corner to help me. To my counsellors and doctors on the Base, I can never say thank you enough.

I SAW A LADY DRESSED IN RED

I saw a lady dressed in red
I knew at once that she was dead.
Her eyes were sunken, skin was grey
I never before saw someone that way.

Bullet casings on the floor
Beside the shoes she'd wear no more
If you ever wonder why I'm blue
Now you see in my mind too.

Images that I can't erase
Cause my heart to beat a rapid pace
For I saw a lady dressed in red
Flies dancing upon her head.

Ethnic cleansing is the work of sick minds. I never understood the concept of wiping out a certain race, religion or creed until Yugoslavia. For a Canadian who lives in a sheltered country with little violence and all of the sudden being immersed in situations where you have to go into places and clean up other people's messes it can be hard to deal with.

I had many friends over my career who have dealt with these situations. No wonder we are fucked up when we get home. For some it's easier to detach and deal with it. Some of us feel helpless at the situation and unable to do anything about it.

I HAD A DREAM

I had a dream of fighting a war
I saw pure hell.
Never the same no more
Death awaiting at every turn
My only thoughts to my kids I return
But when I get home
Sadness and fear.
For I have so much hatred. To all I hold dear.

My soldier's dream is a nightmare so vast
Trapped in pain and anger
Hatred so vast
One can only imagine the terror and fear
When you're so afraid to lose all that is dear.

I finally come home. My mind and heart broke.
My family in shambles.
Nightmares awoke.

I had a dream but did not awake
For I lived this dream
The dream I now shake.

Experiencing first hand the atrocities that some people do to others is a hard thing for some to handle. I had brutal nightmares for a while after my last tour. I remember waking up just drenched in sweat just like I had hopped out of the shower and not dried off.

My dreams were very vivid and always violent. I remember when I was younger having different dreams – now it was all combat, death and destruction. My mind was broken and I could no longer take it any more.

My anger and frustration began to take its toll on not only myself but my family too.

HOUSE UPON A HILL

There was a house upon a hill
There was a cold winter chill
Snow had fallen upon the ground
Where landmines lay all around.

A family sat beside a fire
In the living room where they burned a tire.
Blankets hung where once a wall
Taken down by mortar fall.

Bullet holes ridden the whole house through
Made it very chilly when cold winds blew.
Snuggled up to keep them warm
Still a home but a different form.

There was a house upon a hill
In my mind I picture it still.

I was up in the mountains just outside of a war-torn city. It was mid-November. Snow on the ground. This house I drove by on convoy had the walls blown down by mortars. They had raggedy old blankets hung to stop the wind. They were still living in the house. At least attempting to live in it – I don't know how one would call that living. It was so heart-breaking to see people living in such poor conditions, especially the children.

CONVOY

A country drive
A beautiful site
Up pulls a car glistening white
Window rolls down
Gun comes out
Bullets flying all about
Thankful for the armoured steel
As the driver holds the wheel
The eerie sound of bullets struck
Hard to believe this is my truck.
And as the car pulls away
Thanks for my kevlar vest I pray.

I remember one convoy we did where a car came up beside us and started firing at the hood of the truck. I was too young and inexperienced to fully realize the situation till after. If a bullet fell short, if they switched aim? We lead a sheltered life here in Canada. I have a definite appreciation for home now that I have seen other countries.

RUDE AWAKENING

The camp is dark
All are fast asleep
Except for sentries
At their posts on their feet.
A thunderous boom breaks the night
Silence no longer
Time to fight.
Another boom closer yet
Air raid sirens come on
My boots I get.
A third and fourth bomb
Death is near
Shouting and air raid sirens I hear
Red lights flashing, soldiers scurry about.
Fifth and sixth bomb hit
Even closer no doubt
I'm out of my bed
Got on all my gear.
The seventh and eighth bombs
Bring ringing to my ear
The building shakes
I know it's been struck
Why had I not died
Just a matter of luck.
Time to retreat
The town is lost
I shudder to think
The human cost.

When I was on tour in Yugoslavia we got bombed one night. It was approximately 2 AM. I remember it like it had just happened yesterday. The boom from the bombs hitting. The scramble to get dressed and run to the bomb shelters. A chunk of concrete wall just about took one of my friends' head off. He bent down last minute to put on his boots. If it were not for that, he would have died. It's an experience that is so hard to put into words. The adrenaline hits and you just do what your training commands.

That night after the bombs hit we were evacuated to a British camp down the road. We were there for about a week, then went to another camp. I never saw the village again. I often wonder how the people of that village fared. I felt we should have stayed, fought, protected… but instead we left.

ANGER

So much anger
So much hate
I did not choose
This sickly fate.
My heart is cold
My spirit numb
It's what I do
So I don't succumb
To this hatred
I now hold near
I no longer care
Or hold anything dear
I was the one
Who chose to fight
I feel so numb
Don't know what's right
My spirit broken
My mind is lost
I no longer care about the cost.

I came back off my third tour in 2007. It was a simple tour but for some reason I was so angry at the world. I found that seeing people suffer was so hard on me. I ended up being distant and cold from my family and was so stressed and frustrated that I got angry at the slightest thing. My family and friends just seemed to irritate the crap out of me. My work sucked and my marriage was heading to shit. This point of time was the beginning of my darkest times.

SICKLY SCREAM

A sickly scream
Blood curdling chill
A terrifying dream
My bones a chill
An old lady
A dark night
Cries for her husband
Who lost his life
Cut short of time
This war a crime
And in my slumber
Her pain runs through
Her anguish haunts me
I feel her blue
Never again
Will I stop to dream
Voices reminding me
Of that sickly scream.

While on my tour in Yugo I was on a convoy one day. We stopped just outside a city called Mostar. There was a lady mourning for the loss of her husband who was just killed due to stepping on a land mine. I sat there for what seemed like an eternity listening to her. I could feel her anguish. Her pain and screams haunted me for years.

A LITTLE BOY

A little boy
Looking so tough
Machine gun in hand
Life so rough
Does he really understand
The life he lives
The life he takes
I look at him
My heart breaks
Not even twelve
Long life ahead
If he doesn't wind up dead.
He points his rifle up at me
Will he shoot
Or leave me be?
If he shoots
Can my conscience make
The little boy's life
That I have to take?

While I was in Yugo I had a young kid point a machine gun at me. It was something that I wouldn't have thought much about if it was a soldier because that's what I am.

Being a kid though was harder. What if he shoots? Could I possibly return fire? Could I kill a kid? We are asked to protect ourselves, our convoy and our fellow soldiers from any threat. But what if that threat is a child? How can one deal with those ramifications? I can still see the boy's face sometimes like it was yesterday.

POISON

You are a poison
Rotting my soul
Warping my mind
Help me from this hole.
You help me numb my pain I feel
Keeping me from feelings so real.
But as I slide down your rope
I now begin to lose all hope
When suddenly an angel in my ear
Pulls me from your grasp so dear
Now I am clean
Now I am free
From the poison within me.

When I returned from my last tour I made several wrong choices. I ended up drinking a lot and getting into drugs. It's a choice that I will always wish I could change. At the time I didn't care about anything or anyone, most of all myself.

It was a dark time in my life but with help I made it back. I fought hard for a better life. Did not bury my mistakes but learned from them and made positive changes as a result.

A BLINDING RAGE

A blinding rage
A new age
Turn the page
A calming sound
Noise all around
A way to drown
Sickness that grips
My sanity it tips
Family it rips
My heart aches
The madness breaks
Sanity makes
Peace at last
Haunted by past
Time to hold fast
Death all around
Bodies in the ground
In blood I drown
My eyes they seep
Dreams haunt my sleep
Oh lord, please keep
Another night
Time to fight
No more fright
This anger and fear
Death draws near
... A single tear.

S ometimes in life it's hard to escape from your past. PTSD is an up and down battle of emotions. I remember being happy one minute and angry the next. I would see the news on TV and want to cry.

PTSD

PTSD
Like the trunk of a tree
My mind is twisted
Roots of fear
Hatred grasps me
I love nothing near
My spirit is broken
I twist and I turn
Grown of sickness
My soul does it burn
To war I return
Crazy I'm being
Like the countries I've seen
Roots fester in me
Like the trunk of a tree
Deeper they grow
Dragging me so
As I spiral down
Spin all about
My body shakes
Lunacy no doubt
I long to awake
This sickness I can't shake
I do what I can
But can't break free
Visions that haunt me
This PTSD is killing me.

It's hard for someone to walk a mile in another person's shoes. To understand their thoughts. My thoughts bounced all over. Sometimes trapped in the past or worried about the future. I also had an anger and hatred that ran deep. I got to a point where I felt my family would be better off without me because I felt I caused them so much hurt and turmoil.

I would be out in public and would hear someone's accent or their appearance would remind me of people I dealt with on my tours, and would wrestle with this overpowering urge to beat the crap out of them.

RIVER OF RED

A river of red
Runs through my head
Cold and dead
Thoughts I dread
Blinding crimson
From death I see
Set me free
From this misery.
My sleep is lost
My sanity tossed
Blinding rage
Sets the page
But through the dark
A new spark.

The human body holds a crap load of blood. One does not realize it until you see it in a pool on the ground. For some reason it is one of the images I could not get out of my head. I learned however to deal and talk about the things that bothered me and through that began to heal. With healing I was able to find new direction and new light in my life that had gone dark for so long.

VIOLENCE IN MY MIND

Violent thoughts inside my mind
Visions of death is what I find
Gruesome evil my mind portrays
Will it swallow me whole one day?
Or will it slowly tear apart
My sanity as it has my heart?
Anger bites at every turn
My spirit fights
The fires burn
I feel alone here with my plight
Dreams that haunt me in the night.

I feel I'm going crazy now. I have always been a easy going person but I am home now from my last tour and everything around me drives me nuts. I have violent thoughts running through my head that I don't understand. I am so afraid of losing myself and my family. I wake up in the night drenched in sweat and screaming on the inside. It is a feeling that I can't get past. I feel less of a man due to my inability to get a grip and soldier up.

A GIRL ALONE

A girl alone
Not much but skin and bone
No family or home
Streets she does roam
A girl alone
So ragged and worn
Family dead
Country war torn
A girl alone
Scared as hell
Memories taunt me
I wish her well
Helpless I feel
As I drive away
A girl alone
In my mirror that day.
My convoy moves on
And we roll out of sight
Sadness rips through me
Tears that I fight
A little girl all alone
No family or home
A girl alone
Streets she does roam.

War is fucked up. Especially when it is involving ethnic cleansing. I will never understand humanity's ability to be so cruel. I go overseas to make a difference and when I see how children suffer it rips my heart out.

I saw a little girl once all ragged and torn. I felt helpless and wanted to pick her up and take her home with me. How can people be so cruel and have no regard to how their battles impact children?

VETERAN PLATES

I have veteran plates on my truck
No, I'm not old as fuck
I wasn't in Korea
Or world war two
I did my time
In countries that suck poo.
I wasn't in 'Nam
I have friends that are dead
Taliban can kiss my ass
Fuck you and those rags on your head.
Yugoslavia was living hell
These nightmares I know too well
Israel and Syria are fucked up too
Terrorists, go fuck yourself and your camel too.
I love my country, my family and home
Those other places I will not roam
So if you see me and wonder why
Don't just sneer and pass me by
I have veteran plates on my hog and truck
Please do not question why
Just say thank you for serving and wish me luck.

When I first got my veteran plates on my truck and bike I was so proud. I had a few people comment on why I had them on my truck. I was young. I would never wish to take away from our veterans of WWII and Korea and I thank them for what they have given but I also deserve to display those plates proudly without being questioned or bugged.

And Taliban, al-Qaeda and other terrorists can kiss my ass. If you want to kill someone in the name of your cause please start with yourself and leave innocent people alone.

MY MIND

Fuck my mind
Nowhere to hide
Sometimes I find
Too much anger inside
In such a bind
Get me off this ride
My fucking mind
Spinning inside
Feeling blind
No more pride
My job unkind
My sanity has died
So I say screw you
Politicians lied
They don't care how we do
At least I tried
To make things right
But my mind is fried
Can't sleep at night
Fuck my mind
Nowhere to hide
Sometimes I wish I'd died.

I t's hard feeling like you are on the outside of a glass bottle looking in.
Wanting to change things, I go overseas to help but feel powerless. I return broken and unable to serve. I'm then cast aside. Meanwhile my head is spinning and spiralling out of control. I begin to hate. Anger consumes me. Am I ever to break free?

TERROR AND FEAR

Terror and fear
Draws me near
I feel Death
Hear his breath
My stomach twists
My thoughts list
My mind wanders
My head ponders
Why am I here
Why the fear
Suck it back
Hit the sack
Long day ahead
No more dead
I pray to see
That haunt me.

In the moment of conflict I don't recall feeling fear. It was mainly after the fact that I had to look back and say, "Holy fuck. That was intense." When I was dealing with nightmares that was a different story. I would wake up so gripped with terror. I had a massive fear that my PTSD would consume me and corrupt me. I felt I was slipping toward becoming a dark evil angry man like so many I had encountered.

I wonder if we all fear becoming what we despise most?

A JEEP ON A ROAD

A jeep on a road
Transporting orders its task
Why it was there
None thought to ask
Up to a checkpoint
Body tenses with fear
Guns are drawn out
As the jeep gets near
Without a warning
Not far from sight
Bullets firing
The perilous plight
The driver's thoughts race
Holy crap holy shit
Looks to his right
His friend has been hit
Blood flowing out
Bullets smashing about
As he races away
A bullet goes his way
A burning bite
A terrible blow.
He feels down his back
As blood starts to flow
What do I do
He screams and he shouts
A quick bandage to his friend
To stop blood that pours out
Adrenaline pumping
Four cylinders race
Trying to beat death
Must reach the Base
Pain and agony riddles
But so does his fear
A sigh of relief as the Base does appear
Up to the gate
Last words he hears
We need a medic the guard's words ring out
The next thing you know
The driver passes out.

One of my friends from basic training was shot while I was overseas in Yugo. He was lucky to survive and managed to get to help in time to save his partner's life.

As a soldier we are asked to serve our country. A task we do willingly and with great pride. I have been in dangerous situations several times to protect innocent people from ethnic cleansing, war and terrorist acts. Something I would do again.

FIREWORKS IN THE SKY

Red markers up in the sky
As I sit here listening to bullets fly
Tracers cast eerie glow
As I watch them overhead they go
In the distance battles fought
Terrors that civil war has wrought
With my helmet on I hunker down
As bullets fly all around
To my left and to my right
Land mines fill my every sight
In the distance I hear a boom
Mortar fire and deadly gloom
Gunfire makes a creepy sound
With people dying all around
And now it's time to go to sleep
Nightmares in my mind will creep
And as I sleep the tracers fly
Like fireworks up in the sky.

I remember sitting in a bunker at a checkpoint up in the mountains near Visoko. I would sit at night watching machine gun tracers fly overhead and listen to mortar fire going off in the distance. At the time I didn't pay much attention to it, my mind on my duties. But as you get older you begin to realize that one stray bullet could have impacted your life huge.

THANK THE ANGEL

Thank the angel
Thank my luck
Thankful where
I stopped the truck
I climb on down
From the cab
Another break
The 12-hour trip is drab
My rifle I take
Almost done this trip
I'm very tired
I make a slip
If I were home
Not such a deal
To look where I step
But here it's real

As my combat boot
Hits the ground
I remember then
To look down.
Thank the angel
Watching me tonight
For there is a land mine
An inch to my right
As I stop shaking
I look to the sky
Thank my maker
I'm still alive
'Cause if I had stepped
An inch to the right
This eve would be
My last night.

I was just past Mostar on a convoy. We pulled over for a break on our 12-hour convoy. I was in the co-driver seat. We don't leave the pavement because there are a lot of land mines in the dirt on the side of a road. We are always told to look down before you jump out of the cab but when you've done back-to-back convoys pushing 12-hour days, you get tired.

DEATH

I am like the harbinger of Death
My soul is dark and twisted
As a night shadow
My heart is cold
Like winter's breath
My sanity has listed
I have become shallow
My desire is old
As the evil god Seth
Destruction has visited
My love a barren fallow
Decay clings like rot and mold
I am like the harbinger of Death.

When I was at my worst I felt as if Death and Evil were always going to be present in my life. I was terrified of becoming a monster that I felt I was becoming. I could close my eyes and see horror and ghosts. Gone were the pleasant dreams. Replaced by nightmares.

FREE

If I saw you four years ago
Sitting there that cloth on your head
I'd look at you and wish you were dead
All that I see
Images in my head
Anger and fear
Hatred so dear
But now I am free
I can look at you and smile
My anger and hatred
Been gone for a while
I can shake your hand
Not one bit of hatred
No anger or fear
Cause I'm in my hometown
With those I hold dear
I am finally free
I am finally me.

I have felt the ability to hate people just based on looks or race. It's not something I am proud of. I remember my mom saying one bad apple doesn't necessarily spoil the batch. I now go out of my way to say hi to those who would make my blood boil because I know in my heart that it's not them that have killed my fellow soldiers. A terrorist is exactly that. A monster without morals. To take someone's life is wrong, plain and simple. To do it based on religion or hatred is just evil. I choose to be good and set a positive example for my kids.

AS I LIE

As I lie in bed
So far from home
A distant land
My mind does roam
To the ones
I left behind
Never far
From my mind
As I lie here
And think of you
I wonder if
You think of me too
My kids are safe
With a caring hand
While I'm in hell
This foreign land
Gunfire battles as I sleep
I pray to God
My family keep

A little bear
In my arm held tight
To remind me why
I choose to fight
One piece of home
That keeps you near
Reminds me of
What I hold dear
As I drift
Off to sleep
I pray to God
My sanity keep.

I had a little teddy bear my daughter, Brooklyn, wanted me to bring with me on tour to remind me of home and so I wasn't lonely. It's little things like that that keeps a soldier whole when they are somewhere else. Many nights I lay in bed wondering if my family was ok. It's hard being away but brutal if you are worried about your family.

MOONLIT GLOW

The moonlight casts a creepy glow
Upon white crosses row on row
No names no face
Died for religion or race
No family that will come to weep
Hatred through the land does creep
No one safe within their homes
As soldiers kill all who roams
I wonder in this moonlit night
If God will end this bitter fight
I come from a distant and safe place
Now death and destruction all I face
My tour will end and back I go
To my family that I know
For years I will dream of this plight
Of crosses under moonlit night.

I used to drive a convoy route that had a massive fresh grave site. It was the length of three football fields. Plain white crosses. I knew they were there as a result of ethnic cleansing and war. I am so appreciative of the great country I am from. We never realize how great it is to feel safe until that safety is taken away. I am and always will be proud to be Canadian.

NIGHTMARES UNDONE

I can't awake
This dream I can't shake
Thoughts in my head
Wish I was dead.
Trapped in fear
Death is near
Can not break free
From this misery.
Terror's bitter grasp
Thoughts from my past
Haunt my sleep
Softly I weep.
God I pray
End me today.
Can't eat
I can't sleep.
These nightmares do creep
Can't get out of my head
I wish I was dead.

I can remember waking in the night with vivid terrifying images in my head. So painful are past memories. I am so glad that I can now sleep at night and not wake with thoughts of death and destruction in my dreams. For the longest time I wished for a simple dream of driving a race car or a great fishing trip with my dad.

WHEELS IN MY HEAD

Wheels in my head
Go round and round
My thoughts spinning
Up and down
My mind numb
My gut retched
Spirit dumb
Crazy and fetched
Help me off this train
I need a safer place
Away from this pain
God I beg
Strike me down
I can't handle this spinning
Twisting inside my head
Wheels spinning
Round and round
Crazy slowly go I
As I sit and sigh
God, please
Get this madness from my head
I wish I were dead.

I sometimes felt that I was inside a tornado of twisted thoughts, anger and frustration. My world spinning around me. I could be happy one second then snap into an angered mess the next.

I remember having thoughts so violent that I felt I was going mad. I wanted it to end so much I even planned on running my truck off the jetty into the ocean. I can never express how much I love my family for their understanding or at least trying to understand. :)

SO MUCH RED

I see a jeep
So much red
It paints a picture
In my head
Once green interior
Now stained sickly black
The dried red
From my buddy's back.
Who ever knew
The shades of blue
That go on inside my head
For as I try to sleep
I see so much red
A puddle of dismay
Life gone away
So much red
Inside my head
I think of my friend
Who died that day
A life that's taken
Gone away
Resting now
In an wooden bed
And all I see
Is so much red.

So many lives were lost for the freedom of others. A cost that can't be measured. My heart goes out to their families. I know they were proud to serve as I was.

I watched a friend of mine fall apart from the things he had experienced. At the time I did not realize I was headed down the same path. When we are soldiers we develop such a bond between each other that we are like family. To that end we also share each other's pain.

INNER DARKNESS

Inner darkness
I try to control
Feeling mindless
Out of control
Anger boiling
Frustrations toiling
I need a release
Find some peace
A gun
A knife
Would end this strife.

Peace at last
Maybe so
But 'tis my family
Would suffer so
So off to the gym
Work through this rage
Then to my counsellor
Help turn the page
Out of the darkness
I fight to be
I beg for help
Save me!!!!!!!

Many times I have been so angry that I felt I wanted to hurt someone. A feeling I did not understand. My thoughts to end this insanity in my head run deep. I sometimes feel that my family would be better off without me.

It has been my kids and my family however that have kept me from doing something stupid and selfish. It's not an easy feeling being unable to deal with stress and chaos like a normal person. I feel ashamed, guilty and that I have let my family down.

In these moments I know I need to hit the gym. Blow off some steam and stress, then chat with a close friend or my psychologist.

Then I am mentally re-charged, and not trapped in that inner darkness.

BROWN HAIR AND CURL

I saw a church it had a steeple
I saw that church full of people
I saw those people no life in their eyes
Bodies stiff lots of flies
Why would such a horror exist
In my mind anger it twists.
From my eye's corner a little girl
Pretty dress, brown hair and curl.
Then my thoughts begin to roam
Back to a little girl I left at home.
A beautiful girl with brown hair and curl.
Then my thoughts begin to unfurl
My mind races, my heart weeps
Tears from my eyes softly seep
Suck it back no time for blue
A soldier's job is never through.

I saw a girl remind me of you.
Never have I felt so blue.
As I sit my thoughts begin to roam
Of a little girl
Safe and sound at home.

When I was in Petawawa, Ontario, I made a good friend. I got a phone call about a week after he returned from Rwanda. He was not doing well. He mentioned how he became unraveled when he saw a little girl that reminded him of his daughter. It was not until later in my career that I experienced what he meant. To watch a child suffer is heart wrenching and hard as hell. To make that connection to your own children is brutal. To those who have lost children, my heart goes out to you.

A SOLDIER'S FORTUNE, *Part 2*

A soldier's fortune
I'm finally free
Of all the nightmares that have haunted me.
A soldier's fortune
No more demons from the past
I now can sleep in peace at last.
A soldier's fortune
My kids still love me
Tears of joy fall as I watch them play in a tree.
A career I love
I laugh and I smile
I sing in the shower
Once and a while.
My family and friends
All I hold dear
I love my home town
I'm glad I am here.
A soldier's fortune
I'm free at last
No longer haunted
By demons of past.

The day that you wake up and realize you are finally able to deal with the insanity that was your life. Move on from the wreckage of your lost career, find a new career you are passionate about. Move on from the divorce and start following your own direction. So many vets spiral out of control until they have lost the will to survive. I did not want to be one of those statistical suicides that I watched in the news. I also learned a few great lessons. Tell your kids you are sorry when you screw up. It lets them know it's ok to fail sometimes or to be wrong. The best thing is that you still love them and they you. So many times I was quick tempered and over reacted but when I apologized it made it better. I also needed to find myself again. Learn to laugh and have fun. At first I didn't want to leave the house but after a while of forcing myself it got better. Time to enjoy and appreciate what gifts you have. Life is meant to enjoy.

PART 2

LOVE AND LOSS

THE DANCE

As we dance the dance
Perhaps a chance
To find anew
A love so true
You and I
I dream to fly
To hold you near
Whisper in your ear
Song of your voice
Sounds so sincere
Music drives me
Closer to thee
When I'm with you
I feel free
To dance this dance
Perhaps a chance
A story untold
A love unfold
That magical kiss
Joy and bliss
Your hand in mine
Our bodies entwine
We dance this dance
Perhaps a chance.

I have had a few relationships in my time. When I finally let go of my past and was truly happy and content with myself I met my girlfriend Katherine. I finally felt the confidence that this was the one gal who I was meant to be with. A gal who loved and accepted me the way I was. The dance of courtship is so much like a dance. Be careful where you step, take it slow and easy. Enjoy having your girl in your arms. Appreciate the little steps, do not get too upset when you step on her toes. Try harder next time until you sweep her off her feet.

BEAUTIFUL BLUE

Beautiful blue eyes
Hair strawberry red
A kiss to die for
You're in my head
Beautiful smile
Sweet gentle touch
I wish to hold you
I wish so much
Your voice is alluring
Captivating so
I'll never understand
Why someone would let you go
I wish I was ready
To hold you so tight
To keep you with me
Cold winter nights
Your hair is so silky
So soft does it glow
But I am not ready
It saddens me so
I've been hurt by another
And need time to heal
And you deserve the best
A love that is real.

When you're in transition from heartache to accepting loss, it's hard. Especially when you meet someone you didn't plan on meeting at that time and develop feelings for her. I had someone break my heart and I jumped into dating too quick. Then I met this great gal Katherine who is now my girlfriend. I knew she was sweet, kind and caring. We became friends. At times I wanted more but I was still not ready. Maybe I had been burned too often? Maybe it was fear of being hurt again? All I know is I'm glad she waited till I was ready.

I DREAM OF A GIRL

I dream of a girl
Of love so divine
Glistening hair and skin so fine
A beautiful girl
Not perfectly so
But beautiful to me
A fact she will know.
A beautiful girl with a heart of gold
That I will treasure and worship
As our tales unfold.

I dream of a girl to have and to hold
To snuggle up when nights are cold.
I dream of a girl
Not perfect you see.
I dream of a girl
Who's perfect for me.

I am a hopeless romantic. I would love to find that gal who just takes my breath away. I am not just speaking physical beauty either. It is the whole package that I want. It becomes harder dating as you get older. A guy ultimately just wants to be loved and feel secure. The perfect girl does not exist but perfect for me does. Hope that makes sense.

NEVER AGAIN

Never again will I hurt any more
My bitter heart is out the door
Never again the sweet words spoke
For my heart is now completely broke
Never again a fair maiden's kiss
Never again will I feel such bliss
And as I lie here unable to sleep
Tears from my eyes begin to seep
As pain and agony draws me near
Your voice fades from my ear.
Never again I'll feel such loss
For my heart will pay the cost.
Never again.

I wrote this just after my girl broke up with me. I was crushed and devastated. I felt at the time I had never loved someone so much. It felt like I was gonna puke. I felt at the time that I would never love again. I had been in a few relationships prior that did not work and was contemplating whether it would be worth it to just be single.

MY HEART IS LOCKED

My heart is locked.
Chained in a box.
I've been hurt before and will no more.
Only a special girl will have the key
When she unlocks she will set it free
For my heart has been broken
It's damaged and scarred
It still works although beaten and marred.
So I put it in a box with walls that are thick
I then buried it in a hole and covered it with mortar
    and brick.
One day I will find a gal that loves me so fine
To her I will serve
A heart that is mine.
Thus doing so she will feel a love so like never before
    and then I pray my heart aches no more.
I offer my heart
And then never again
For it has been broken too often
Next time it won't mend.

Heartache is one of the most shitty feelings that I think I have faced. Dating in your 40s you think would be easier but I actually found it harder. Not only are you finding someone right for you but you also have to find a person who will accept your kids as well. My wife left me a few years after my last tour. I had a few shitty relationships at this point and had been dumped a few tines because certain gals felt I had no room in my life for them with my three kids. I learned that it was definitely their loss.

PIECE BY PIECE

Piece by piece my heart breaks
Piece by piece there is no more
A broken shell
An empty room without a door
Bit by bit I die a death
A thousand times like never before
But out of the ashes I shall rise
My heart broken no surprise
My heart locked up like never before
Locked in a box so I'll hurt no more
But someday I hope to give anew
My heart to one who will be true
One who deserves such a gift
For her my heart out of this box I'll lift.

I have gone through a lot of trials in life. Heartbreak is a tough one. I have built walls so that no one ever will be able to cause me such pain again. But I am not the type to stay behind walls. I wish for that one gal who will someday come who will appreciate me for who I am.

I TRUSTED YOU

I trusted you
You lying whore
You're such a bitch
We are no more
I would have gave you
My all, my life
But you had to stab me
With that knife
My heart will heal
Finances lost
But everyone knows
'Tis you that paid the cost
You're an evil bitch
So much is true
But I can rest
I know you're due
Karma will bite you
In the ass
Cause you fucked me over
In the past.

I dated a girl who was very dishonest, manipulative and downright evil. Trust is something that most people like to give until there is a reason not to. Unfortunately I met someone who was evil enough to lie about her father's death to manipulate me. I learned a lot from that experience.

AS I SIT

As I sit
I wonder why
Has my life
Just passed me by
The life I live
Have I more to give?
Do I try
Can I forgive?
Sometimes I cry
My heart captive
Love is a lie
A drowning sieve
My faith would die
Must I be festive?
Give it another try?
As I sit
I ponder why.

I have gone through a lot of heartache and pain in my life. Sometimes in life I have felt what's the point. I remember my dad saying, "If it weren't for bad luck, I'd have no luck at all."

I have to take a step back at times and realize life is not always easy. Sometimes we feel it's just us getting crapped on but we are all in it. I have learned money is only money. It's family and friends that are important.

FALLING

I'm falling for you
Yes, it's true
I'm full of joy
No longer blue
My walls are crumbling
I know it so
My heart is melting
Like springtime snow
Your beautiful smile
And gentle touch
Makes me want you
Near so much
I think of you often
Want to hold you tight
Curl up beside you
All through the night
As I slowly
Drift off to sleep
My heart is warm
Thoughts of you I keep.

The moment you realize you have fallen for someone can be great but it can also be scary as hell. Love has the ability to rise above all or cut you down and leave you a shredded mess. Some people choose to give up and stay single. Me, I have always been too stubborn to give up on anything without a fight. Some things are worth it.

AS I LIE AND THINK OF YOU

As I lie I think of you
Of what we had
Between us two
I've shed my tears
No longer sad
Once hurt we were through
Now kinda glad
Through all the years
I drove you mad
Through all the times
I made you sad
Our life's blurred lines
That we have had
All our bad times
When I was angry and mad
And for those times
I'm sorry I made you sad
As I lie and think of you
I hope you're happy
And no longer blue.

P TSD is a family disease. My anger, terror and fear is so apparent to my family and affects them all. I can only imagine how hard it was for them to sit back and watch when I was filled with so much anger and hate. The many times I would snap and lose my temper. Many times I felt my family would be so much better off without me. I often wished I had died overseas and saved my family the pain and suffering I now felt I put them through. So many veterans commit suicide because we can't cope and feel alone and isolated. I am so thankful I realized that was not so.

I LOST

I lost my dream
It's gone I fear
Quite unreal it seems
Through all the years
My visions lean
So many tears
Sometimes it's serene
The unwavering rears
I wish it was foreseen
My thoughts a sphere
Become very obscene
The concept so sheer
My dream is pristine
Something to adhere
Like a ship I must careen
Or my dream will disappear.

I have felt so often that my dream has been lost. No longer on the path I wanted my life to be on. I never pictured that I would be divorced. I always wanted the family, nice house and to be happy. My career I loved taken away and no idea what to do next.

I WANT YOU

I want you
I want your sweet caress
Your gentle touch
I want you a little
I want you very much
I want you close
I want you near
I want your voice
Whispering in my ear
I want your soft hands upon mine
I want your lips so divine
I want you in my arms
Hold you tight
I want you beside me through the night.
I want you.

Those first months of dating are great. The rush you get when you are around that person. It's a great feeling to be around that special gal. To have someone you feel secure with.

YOU'RE IN MY HEART

You're in my heart
That you tore apart
You're in my dreams
So sad it seems
All the tears
All the fears
Memories fade
Like a bill that's paid
No longer blue
That I've lost you
Time to walk away
Live for a new day
New love will bring
Songbirds that sing
But one thing is true
I always hold a piece of you
In my heart
That you tore apart.

I have had my heart ripped out and I would not wish that on anyone. I would rather go through severe physical pain than have my heart broken. Physical wounds heal quick.

Heartache will heal over time but it feels like forever.

A PILL

If there was a pill to erase my mind
Your memories would be hard to find
If there was a pill to erase my pain
My love for you has nothing to gain
If there was a pill to hide my tears
I would no longer have all these fears
If there was a pill to forget your kiss
Then my dear I would not miss
If there was a pill to forget your hug
Then when I'm lonely it would not bug
If there was a pill to wipe images of you
My wish will finally have come true
If there was a pill to drown our past
My heart would be free at last
If only there was a pill
Then my stomach would not feel so ill.

We all wish there was that magic little pill to erase our fears, pain and heartache. Sometimes we would love to forget certain people were even in our lives. Erase all memory. But would that help? At the time it doesn't seem like it, but we grow with our pain.

RENT

You rent a spot
Inside my head
I feel so numb
My heart is dead
I want to go
Find something new
I question so
Will it ever be true
Will I find
My one true love
Am I blind
I ask God above
Or am I destined
To live in pain
I give so much
Have I nothing to gain?

Heartache sucks ass. To lose someone you love is not easy to get over. Time will heal but it is a long road. I have loved and lost. I someday hope I find the special one I will grow old with.

LOVE

Love is a river
Winding and twisting
Until it reaches the sea
Sometimes love makes you shiver
Like a cold wind whistling
But it is a great gift to see.

Love is a bird soaring in flight
Love can be magic
Love comes in spurts
Sometimes in love you will fight
Love can be tragic
Sometimes love hurts.

Love will enhance
Like making a cake
It takes time and work
You have to take a chance
Jump in and bake
Love has its perks.

Love is a flower
Beautiful and pure
With sunlight and care
Love will give you power
Love is a great cure
Love is not bare
Love makes you care.

Love is a precious gift. Those who squander it away will someday realize they have lost one of the greatest things in life that they could have. My cousin Jason recently got married. You could tell how much he and his wife loved each other. It was great to see.

FIREFLY DANCING

A dance in the night
A beautiful sight
A fiery glow
Tangle and flow.
Intricately weaving up and down
Like fireflies dancing all around
A courtship ritual
A magical dance
Is she the one
I ponder the chance
A gentle touch
A warm embrace
Your beauty brings a smile to my face
Sweet words spoken
A gentle kiss
My mind flows with joy and bliss
A beautiful creature
You are to me
A firefly dancing
Under a tree.

I remember as a child heading to a jamboree in Guelph, Ontario with my scout troop. We stopped in this campground in Ontario. I saw fireflies in the field. We even caught a few and put them in jars. They were magical. I feel the same with dating that special someone. A courtship ritual of colour and dance.

I remember the Blue Bayou Restaurant at Disneyland. My parents took me there when I was young. There was a lagoon setting with fake firefly lights all around. I would love to see that again.

DEWDROPS ON A ROSE

Dewdrops on a rose
Teardrops falling on my toes
Something beautiful
Something lost
My heart breaks
My will is tossed
I'm so sorry
You'll never know
How much I loved you
I'll never show
This last tear I shed for you
Reminds me of a drop of dew
Crashing down upon a rose
For I loved you more than anyone knows.

In life we sometimes forget the greatest gifts we can get is someone's love. It is supposed to be unconditional and timeless if you are with the right person. When one person feels different it is hard to accept. As time moves on and you find the right one, it's great.

IF YOU ONLY KNEW

If you only knew
Why my heart is blue
Then you would understand
Why I am the way I am
My heart hurts
My tears flow
I never knew I could hurt so
My thoughts of you
With another man
Crush my heart
And twist my soul
I am a wreck
A twisted heap
But I will attempt another leap
For out of the fire
Burns anew
I will find a love that's true.

When I lost a gal I thought was the right one I was a wreck. I had to take time to figure out who I was and what I truly wanted. I am so lucky I have now found such a great gal whose heart matches her beauty.

I FELL IN LOVE WITH YOU

I fell in love with you
I really wish it wasn't true
As these tears hit the floor
I await the day I cry no more
I loved your laugh
I loved your smile
Your gentle touch
I'd walk a mile
Long to hold you
Squeeze you tight
Keep you warm on cold nights
But you moved on
And left me blue
But I'll never regret
Loving you.

Never regret our past loves, laughter or mistakes. It's how we grow. Without first experiencing pain and suffering I sometimes wonder if I would really appreciate what I have.

The heart is a complex organ. Who would ever know it could break or be ripped out? I have definitely felt it has been torn from my chest. Or was it all in my head?

I'VE LOVED

I've loved
I've lost
I've paid the cost
I've sang
I've danced
I took a chance
I have hurt so much
My heart is numb
Sometimes I feel
Love is dumb
Not sure I can
Live this way
If I lose love
Another day
For I've loved
I've lost
My heart's paid the cost.

My thoughts of love and heartache have always been deep. I have a huge heart. The downside is it can get hurt easily. The plus side is that special gal who appreciates it will never feel unloved.

NOT ANOTHER TEAR

I will not shed another tear
What we had was very dear
Although it pains me
Very so
I have to let my love go
Pictures and memories of the past
Dwindle and fade
A love died at last
As I sit
As I dream
My tender thoughts
Dwindle it seems
Your smiles
Your kiss
Fade into past
My love for you dies at last
I will not shed another tear
For I'll keep them for someone
Someone that's dear.

Freedom comes when you finally reach that moment after a heartache or lost love that you know you are over being sad. The moment where you realize that not another tear will be shed for that person is like a breath of fresh air. Remember the past, both good and bad. However, don't let it hold you back or make you bitter. If that happens, you have truly lost.

SLOWLY

Slowly I die inside
My heart withers
My pain I can't hide
My thoughts give shivers
I'm twisted and wrought
Without you my thought
My stomach is ill
If there was a pill
To remove all the pain
I have nothing to gain
God I beg
End it now
Make me love,
No more somehow
As I sit alone tonight
I wish I could
End my plight
My mind unravelled
Say it ain't so
Why, oh why
Did you have to go?

S ome things in life need little explanation. This poem was a memory of how I once felt. Since then I have grown and realized what I truly want out of life.

Which is surprisingly pretty simple.

LIPS OF AN ANGEL

Lips of an angel
Pressed to mine
So divine
Sweet and soft
My thoughts aloft
My mind races
My spirit soars
As I kiss you
At your front door
Lips of crimson
Gentle and sweet
The first time
Our lips meet
Taste of honey
Soft as hell
Your sweet lips
Cast their spell.

The first kiss from that special girl can be magical. It's a nerve wracking experience as well though. What if it isn't good? What if she pulls away? Then what do you do? I have always been a bit daft on reading cues from girls. I remember reading somewhere, "Hints do not work with me, even obvious ones. If you want me to do something, ask."

I MISS YOU

I miss you
I am so blue
I miss your touch
I want it so much
But as time passes
Your memory fades
Your face blends into the masses
Your image shades
My heart withers
My spirit dies
Like a burned out shell
I tell no lies
My loneliness is hell
The flames of rejection
Catch me for a spell
A dying desire
Burns like fire
But as time passes
I find this true
I miss you less
I am not blue
There is resurrection
From out of the fire
There burns anew
Another desire
I'll find someone
Who loves me true.

They say the quickest way to get over someone is to meet someone new. I did that when I was younger but as I grew up I realized that serial dating was not helping me. The heart needs time to mend broken pieces otherwise you are just hurting someone who doesn't deserve it.

TWISTED

My thoughts are twisted
Confused as fuck
My life with love
I've had little luck
When I look at you
I want to smile
And hold you tight
All the while
But my heart is broken
I see no end
My twisted heart
Has yet to mend
I want to hold you
I want your touch
But my heart is hers
It hurts so much
For she does not want me
I don't understand
It pains me so
Seeing her with that man
As I lie here
I think of my plight
How it would feel
To be with you tonight.

When the girl you feel at the time is the love of your life is suddenly with another guy it can drive you insane. Lost sleep. Bouts of sadness claw at your sanity. Then you finally meet someone who is great. When you look at her you not only see outer beauty but inner beauty as well. The only issue, someone else still holds a piece of your heart. You want to be with this new gal, however your insanity still draws you to the past. It's like being pulled between two poles. When is the time to move on? Try to break free from the insanity and let your heart guide you.

SHE LOVES ME, SHE LOVES ME NOT

You tell me you love me
Then you go
Mental bullshit
I don't know
You tell me you love me
Then you walk away
You rip my heart out
Then ask me to stay
You draw me near
Then shut me out
You're fucking crazy
There is no doubt
You tell me you love me
But just as a friend
But friends care
To this there is no end
You tell me you love me
But act like you don't care
Your mind is broken
Your heart is bare
Cold and selfish
I'm blunt but true
Hurt by another
So you hurt me too
You tell me you love me
But hurt from your past
So I shall move on
And leave this at last.

A BEAUTIFUL ROSE

You are like a beautiful rose. Captivating
to look at. Soft and delicate, yet strong
and alluring. Lips like the crimson red
of the flower. Skin so satin soft and
delicate like the touch of the petals.
How I long to hold you close and kiss
you gently.

How can a beautiful flower hold so much
within? Beauty, Warmth, Happiness
and Joy. You make me laugh. You make
me smile. You bring me to the edge of
desire and back. My inner child bursts
forth. My desires are fulfilled. Never
have I longed so much for another.

A flower in any form can't hold a candle
to your ability to captivate my mind, my
heart and my body. You are desirable
and sweet. It is like you were sent from
the heavens for me.

Every time I see a beautiful rose I am
reminded of you.

HUMMINGBIRD

You are like a hummingbird
Loose in my heart
Beautiful colour flittering all over
Spreading warmth and joy when I
    close my eyes
All I see is crimson and emerald
    green in your thoughts
Painting memories of your beauty
Darting here and there imprinting me
    with your touch
How I long to hold you
How I long to make you mine
I am captivated by you.

BRICK WALL

I built a wall
So no one gets in
It's very tall
Protected within
I'm safe inside
No more sin
The place I hide
Trapped in a bin
Get off this ride
Stubborn pride
Anew I begin
A brick wall.

There comes a point in life where you just want to lock your heart away. No more searching for the right one. No more heartache. No more tears. Put defences up so no one gets close. That way no one has the ability to hurt you anymore.

I THINK OF YOU

I think of you
Of our first kiss
The thought brings
Joy and bliss
I long to hold you
And squeeze you tight
Wish you here
With me tonight
In my arms
Safe and sound
The smiles you bring
Laughter abound
I think of you
Of our first kiss
When you're not here
It's you I miss.

When I sit alone at night my house is so quiet. Sometimes it's very peaceful and relaxing but I always wish my girlfriend Katherine was there with me.

PART 3

SHIT THAT MAKES ME SMILE

SHITTY POETRY

As I sit and shit
I hear a plop
I ponder and stop
I think of life
And the shit gone through
A shitty life?
Not really, You?
Times were tough
Sometimes hard
I've had it rough
Acted like a tard
But through the years
Two things hold true
My friends were there to dry the tears
Give me hugs
And help with fears
And when I poo
I think of you.

This was just a goofy one I made while I was bored. Not too hard to figure out what I was in the middle of. Some people have the ability to pop in your head at the weirdest times.

BEAUTIFUL ROSE

Beautiful rose
It knows
No boundaries
Nothing shows
But beauty so alluring
Vibrant in colour
Rich in life
Softer than the softest skin
Fragrant scent deep within
Beautiful rose
Knows not how
To love or to hate
Or fear somehow
As morning dew
Drops within
Beautiful rose
Glistening skin
A thing of God's beauty
Shimmering glow
Was it intended to be so
Did only God know
Or merely a flower
Beautiful rose
That grows where it grows.

I was on my coffee break one day and there were rose bushes outside at work. I have always liked roses. The sweet smell and they are very nice to look at. My favourite would be the blue ones you see at Cosco once in a while. For some reason I have always liked them.

IF FISH COULD DRIVE A BOAT

If fish could drive a boat
Would it float?
Would it sail?
Or would they bail?
I laugh and try
To reason why?
If fish could fly?
Or would they try?
Can they drive a car?
Would they go far?
In a spaceship perhaps
To touch a star?
Or ride a bike?
Perhaps a pike?
Riding a trike
A funny thought
With laughter I'm wrought.

This is the number two instalment of poems that I wrote for my little guy. I want to have my kids remember to laugh and have fun. I have wasted so much time worrying about things I have no control over. I want them to remember the laughter, silliness and little moments.

CHRISTMAS CHEER

On this night of Christmas cheer
I now shed a single tear
No more children dancing about
For a zombie horde is out!
The bastards have brought Santa down
There are no more toys in this town
Then I feel another tear
The fuckers ate Santa's reindeer!
And if you wonder why I'm blue
The bastards got the Easter Bunny too.
On this night of Christmas cheer
I see a zombie eating Rudolph's ear.
Christmas will never be the same
Now it will be so fucking lame.

My favourite movies are zombie movies. I am a huge fan of the walking dead. I often drive my daughter Brooklyn nuts with my Facebook posts because I'll see a cool pic of a 4x4 truck with a machine gun mounted on it or cool swords and I'll post it and say that it would be great for when the zombie apocalypse hits.

A SOLITARY ROSE

A field of grain
In sunshine it glows
Wind whistles by
It ebbs and it flows
And in that grain
A single wild rose
How it got there
God only knows
When I picture that rose
My mind it appears
Flowing red curls
Blue eyes so sincere
Longing to hold
But ridden with fear
Sweet crimson lips
Soft fingertips
A smile in a way
That brightens your day
In a field of grain
A solitary rose
How it got there
God only knows.

Through all my travels I have seen some wonderful things. Some just take your breath away. Such beauty – how does it exist? How does it survive in such a hungry world that devours all in its path.

I saw a rose once in a field. The grain was golden. Glistening in the sun and gently swaying in the wind. It reminds me of beauty. Kind and gentle.

A FIELD OF GRAIN

A field of grain
Gentle it flows
Moving in the rain
Back and forth it goes
Just like life
Lessons it shows
Back and forth it goes
Like life's ups and downs
In the storm it blows
Beauty can be found
Through storm and strife
The musical sound
Look for the beauty in life
Like a field of grain
Even in the darkest night
Beauty is found
Just look for the light.

I was driving back for my coffee break from a job and in the field I was passing I saw a field of grain. Golden and waving in the sun.

As I ponder my life I have had several ups and downs but I can always take beauty and something good out of every situation. You just have to look for it. Doing this I have found that the little moments in life meant more than the bad stuff and I have become more appreciative and happy.

RAINDROPS ON TIN

Raindrops on a tin roof
Magical sound
Falling down
Living proof
On the ground
That calming sound
Smashing on the tin
Pitter patter
Dance begin
Takes you away
To a distant place
No fear or anger
A beautiful space
Worries dance away
Lost in a trance
Magical array
Raindrops on tin
Life begin.

I grew up in a trailer and one of the sounds that I love to this day is listening to a heavy rain beating on the tin roof. It's so relaxing and magical. I have a tin roof on the back of my porch that my dad helped me build. I will always think of my dad when I hear that. It reminds me of the times when I was younger, having my dad teach me things like working on cars. *Dad, I love you. You have always been there for me and have always been my hero.*

WHY DOES THE DOG BARK?

Why does the dog bark?
Every time we're at the park
He barks when he sees a plane
He barks when he sees a train
He barks at cars
Would he bark on Mars?
I wonder why it's so?
Why do they bark at cars?
He barks when people come
He barks when people go
He barks at some
And sometimes no
Is he just dumb
I wonder it so?

I have written a couple of poems for my kids. I love to see them laugh and have fun. It's great when you get to have goofy moments and make them smile.

BEARS DANCE

Out in the woods I run into a bear
I am not frightened
I am not scared
I laugh so hard
What's the chance
I see bears dancing in their underpants?
Out in the woods on a scary night
I see bears dancing under moonlight
You would think I'd worry running into a bear
But I saw them dancing in their underwear
I laughed so hard
What's the chance
Of seeing bears dancing in their underpants?
Big ones, small ones
Without a care
Bears dancing in their underwear
Skinny ones, fat ones
Crazy as a bat ones
I did not worry
I did not care
Funny to see a bear
Dancing in his underwear.

I wrote this for my son. He has a goofy sense of humour just like his dad. :)
I could probably write a book on the funny things he has come up with.
Forever the class clown. He is always trying to make people laugh. I guess
he comes by that honestly.

ZOMBIES ATTACK

When zombies attack late at night
Get ready to run
Get ready to fight
Grab your sword and gun
When zombies attack you might be done
They have no mind
Rotting corpse with no soul
A killing machine that knows no other role
They will claw and bite
Cause a dreadful fright
Tear off chunks of your skin
Then evil you turn within
You lose all your thoughts
Love and memories are wrought
Evil surges within
Drive for eating flesh will begin
An empty shell you will be
Driven mad to eat the kid in the tree.

SCRATCHING AT THE DOOR

I hear scratching at the door
Not my dog I have no more
In the distance screams and shouts
For this night are zombies about
Safe inside with my kin
Hoping that the zombies don't get in
Right next door awful sounds
I realize their door has come down
All I hear are cries and screams
As zombies have their feast it seems
Something at my door wants in
An evil dead drive for flesh within
I have a large bat with spikes in hand
I am ready for a stand
If zombies break in
They will not pass.
I'll go Genghis Khan on their ass.

Another zombie poem. I often wonder what it would be like if the
dreaded zombie apocalypse hit? I know, what a geek, huh? My kids
got me a zombie statue with a Canucks jersey on it for Xmas. I would love
to see someday how they do the makeup for the walking dead. Love that
show too. :)

FRIEND

You pick me up
Wipe my tear
You're in my heart
I hold you dear
I'm glad we met
My life I bet
Has a ray that shines
Through all that binds
You see past the dark
Make my spirit shine
I'm so glad
My friend
You're mine
Sadness and fear
Dwindle when you're near
We talk
We laugh
I'm honest
And true

A long time each other
Would think we knew
Although we have only
Been friends a while
You have a way
To make me smile
As I ponder
I think this true
I could never ask
For a better friend
Than you.

I have had the pleasure of having some great friends in my life and I love them all. I would do so much for my friends. It's great when you have those special friends that know you. That you can be honest with and not afraid to show your real self.

NEW INK

The buzzing of the gun
Exhilaration and fun
Needles scratching at my skin
Leaving ink deep within
Art of a different form
Leaves me all giddy and warm
Watching a masterpiece unfold
A new story or terror told
As I look at the blood leak out
Adrenaline rushes I want to shout
Pain and pleasure mixing about
As a new picture takes its hold.

I remember my first tattoo when I was 21. I said I only wanted the one. Now I have eleven and want more. It's totally addicting. My folks keep telling me, "That's nice, dear, but we think you have enough."

Can you ever have enough? ;)

BIKER POEM

If you were to see me on the street
I don't wear a suit
But I'm clean and neat
Even though you may not want to say hi
I will nod and smile as you walk by
I have tattoos and piercings on my skin
Some people think I live a life of sin
Pictures of skulls cover my arms like a cast
To remind me of death I faced in the past
To my family and friends I'm loyal and true
But I may look like a gangster biker to you
I would be the first to lend a helping hand
For I've a heart of gold you can understand
I would lay down my life for my kids or my wife
Face death and destruction from gun or knife
So think twice before judging
How I look
Cause I'm a good person don't judge me
    like the cover of a book.

When I got out of the military I wanted to grow a goatee and get my ears pierced. I also wanted more ink. I developed a love for skulls, zombies and anything with a dark side. Not too sure why, maybe to remind me how precious life is. Maybe because I felt so dark inside that I can relate.

A LITTLE SWIFT

A little bird
Delicate and sweet
Songs of joy
Delicate feet
Your song is sweet
A beautiful sight
To see God's gift
And watch your flight
I sit and watch
You out my door
A delicate bird
That flies and soars
As I sit and watch
My mind it drifts
What would it be like
To live life as a swift
To soar and fly
No care as why
Twisting and turning
Flying like mad
My question to you
Is a swift ever sad?

Have you ever just sat and watched Nature and appreciated the simple gifts we have? I am fortunate to live in such a beautiful country filled with wonder and beauty. With the help of my counselling I have learned to finally stop and appreciate such a gift.

A WINDING COUNTRY ROAD

A winding country road
Frost on the ground
No cars to be found
Peaceful and quiet
Tranquil and serene
I take in the scene
On the throttle grips
Adrenaline rips
At one with the road
Nothing around
My hog the only sound
A country road
Peaceful and sweet
Escape from the street
Peace in my mind
Relaxation I find.

I am fortunate living in Victoria where I can ride my Harley all year around. I remember when I was young. My dad had a couple of old bikes that my friends and I used to rip around on. A Honda Trail 90, and a big red trike. I have always loved motorcycles. When I was getting out of the Forces I finally had the cash to buy my Harley. I find it so relaxing, especially on some of the back roads around Victoria area.

PART 4

A NEW DAY

Writing this was so hard for me. I grew up with few good memories of my mother. I learned at a later age that my grandfather on my mom's side was a sick abusive ass. My mom went through hell as a child. Unfortunately, the cycle did not end there. My mother learned the wrong lessons from her father. These are the feelings I grew up having. For the longest time I blamed my First Nations heritage. If my dad and step mom were not there for me when I was growing up I would probably have ended up in jail.

We don't seem to appreciate our parents until we are older. It wasn't until I was older that I started understanding and seeing the bigger picture.

I now embrace my heritage and see the beauty in it. That's what I choose to pass on to my kids. Domestic violence and alcohol abuse are not acceptable. It's time to break the cycle and embrace our positive heritage. The beauty of our art and culture. Not be dragged down by our demons.

The greatest gift my mother gave me other than life was the day she came to me and said she was so sorry for what she had done. Her apology helped me move on and meant so much to me. I was so torn as to put this poem out there. I do not wish to hurt my mom. I grew up being so angry with my mother. It's not how a child is supposed to feel. I wrote this so people would stand up against violence and abuse. *Mom, I forgive you and love you. The past is in the past. It's time to forgive yourself and move on.*

MOTHER

Mother, you're sick
Twisted and ill
You need help
Take a fucking pill
You're supposed to be caring
Lend a helping hand
Not beat the shit out of me
Cause I remind you of Dad
A board with nails
A frying pan
Chose your weapon, bitch
I don't understand
Your not caring
You're evil and mean
That's why I left home
A change of scene
A two by four
Across my back
No wonder I have issues
Intimacy I lack
My body is scarred
My mind black and blue
You were a shitty mother
But your father did this to you
Time to break the cycle
No looking back
I will not beat my children
Love they will not lack.

THE CYCLE WILL BREAK

The cycle will break
Like pieces of glass on the floor.
This hatred I shake
Like these feelings I feel no more.

My heart is lifted
Peace at last
I feel gifted
No fear of the past.

I shed a skin
I walk away
No hatred within
Live a new day.

The circle is broken
My song is new
I've lifted the hatred
That haunted you.

When you have experienced a home full of abuse, it is so hard not to walk down the same path. We don't realize the affect parents have on their children until we are grown. I grew up with two homes – one was dysfunctional and one normal. My dad and step mom showed me a better path. If it were not for them I doubt I would be the man I am today. It takes a very special lady to love and care for another's child as if he were her own.

I know that my mother loved me. She always has. But there is a cycle that for some it's hard not to repeat what we were taught at a young age.

I wrote this for those who have broken that cycle and who try to give their kids a life of love and happiness that they deserve. Children are truly our greatest gift and accomplishment.

I MET A GIRL WITH A HEART OF GOLD

I met a girl with a heart of gold
I met a girl I want to hold
I met a girl with a Midas touch
I met a girl I love so much
I met a girl with the sweetest kiss
I met a girl causes me bliss
I met a girl that makes me smile
For this girl I'd walk a mile
I met a girl with a heart of gold
I want to hold when nights are cold
I met a girl who loves me so
A girl that I will not let go.

I have dated a lot since my wife left. I have met some decent gals and some that I really wish karma would bite in the ass. Hard, multiple times.

I finally met a girl with a kind genuine heart.

A FATHER'S GIFT

A father's gift
He has to hold
Worth more than oil
Or silver and gold

A father's gift
Worth more than fortune or fame
It's very grand
Not at all lame

A father's gift
To this I hold true
Can't be measured by riches
It doesn't come in blue

A father's gift
Sometimes makes you cry
That gut wrenching moment
When you kiss them goodbye

A father's gift
All peaceful at sleep
Snuggled in bed
Such angels they sleep

A father's gift
Beautiful and bright
To watch them grow up
I hope I did it right?

A father's gift
The best love of all
A child's love
The greatest gift of all.

I have been given many things in life. But I must say the greatest gift has been my children. I love them with all my heart and would do anything for them. I've watched them grow; sometimes I wish they would stop growing, just to preserve the moment.

LIFE

I've loved
I've lost
I've sang
I've danced
I've even wore women's underpants
I've kissed a dude
I've acted rude
I've been kind
Been kinda blind
I've angered
I've cried
I've wish I'd died
I've made mistakes
I've baked a cake
I've felt blue
I've been true
I've cheated Death
I've felt his breath.

I spent almost 20 years in the Canadian Forces. I have seen approximately 18 different countries. I have experienced so much through my life. This poem was just a touch of what I have gone through and a summary of most people's lives.

THE FIRST TIME

The first time
I held you
I knew our bond
Would always hold true
The first time
I held you
In my arms
I knew I would
Be weak to your charm
I knew at once
I'd love you so
Now it's time to let you go
All grown up
Out to the world
You'll always be
My little girl.

My oldest daughter used to have the cutest little brown curly hair. She melted my heart the first time I saw her. We have had our share of experiences. Trips to the hospital, conversations with teachers, groundings and late nights worrying about missed curfews. In the end it's great to see her grow up, graduate and become such a beautiful young lady. In my heart you will always be Daddy's little girl. :)

A NEW DAY

A new day
Come my way
No time for fears
Only joy
No tears
A new smile
A new kiss
Magical moments
Joyful bliss
Heart pounding
Music sounding
Filling my soul
Where once a hole
A new day
A song
A dance
A new chance
Sun rises
Night fall
A new story
I live it all
New surprises
A sweet wine
A new day
And I'm feeling fine.

The joy that you feel when you can wake up having a full night's sleep is great. I can go into a mall and not worry about someone setting off a bomb. I can sit in heavy traffic and not be looking for a car to come up shooting. I'm always going to have memories and anxiety but I can now deal with them.

I am free to live and enjoy life.

A BEAUTIFUL FLOWER

A beautiful flower
Knows no part
Except a little piece of the heart
A single petal leaves no trace
As does a single embrace
Like a withering petal falls to the floor
An embrace fades to feel no more?
But a springtime flower buds anew
Bursting forth colour vibrant and true
A beauty that leaves a tale unfold
Reminds of love so beautiful and bold
As a field of tulips grow so vast
Erasing decay that comes from a past
A springtime flower buds at last.

Life can sometimes be compared to growth of a flower. Sometimes it withers and dies like friendships, jobs, etc. But if you feed the roots with positivity, happiness and love, new flowers will grow. I have found that just because I have dealt with rough times, death and decay, it does not mean that I give up and wither and die myself. I have seen the most beautiful flowers grow in the most inhospitable places. This teaches me that just because things are rough does not mean to give up.

PART 5

PHOTO GALLERY THEN AND NOW

Above: *Gunner Seivewright and myself. We were on our way for a winter indoctrination exercise in Arctic Bay, Northwest Territories. Our plane had to do an emergency landing in Trenton, Ontario due to a hydraulic fluid leak causing us to miss the first few days of the exercise. The weather was -50° to -70° with wind chill. We had to build our own igloo and sleep in it one night.* Below: *Winged Dagger Exercise. I was securing the landing zone while the rest of my battery landed by helicopter. Just one of the many field exercises I did while with the Artillery.*

Above left: *This was one of the M109 self-propelled Howitzers that I operated while with 2nd Regiment Royal Canadian Horse Artillery.*
Above right: *A convoy through Bosnia. One of the many typical convoys I was on while over in the former Yugoslavia. For part of my tour I was attached to the RCD battle group. Below: Exchange program. We were hosting Artillery from Norway. This photo was taken at a mess dinner.*

Top: *Photo was taken after completion of basic training at CFB Cornwallis. I was 21.* Middle: *I took this shot inside a small church. It was hard to feel like there was a God or much good anywhere, when we were surrounded by war and ethnic cleansing.* Below: *A small church in former Yugoslavia. There was a huge hole in the side of the wall where a mortar hit it.*

Top: *This was what was left of a home in Bosnia after being battered by mortar and gun fire. It was a common sight to see a few houses untouched then one completely destroyed.* Middle: *When I was in Visoko we had a bomb dropped on our camp. We evacuated down the road to a Brittish camp. This picture was of me chatting with a Brittish soldier and we were checking out each other's weapons.* Below: *Taking a break on the first stage of a twelve-hour convoy from Primosten, Croatia into the Bosnian Mountains past Visoko.*

Above: *My oldest daughter, Amanda, at age 2.5 years old and at 4 years old.* Left: *Amanda and my youngest, Jacob, ages 18 and 8.* Below: *This photo is of my daughter, Brooklyn, and me. It was taken at my cousin Jason's wedding. I was 43 and Brooklyn was 14.*

Above: *Brooklyn, Jacob and me at Witty's Lagoon, Victoria, BC, summer 2013.* Inset: *Brooklyn and Jacob late at night walking on the beach.* Below left: *Jacob and Brooklyn, spring 2012, riding on their chopper out front of the house.* Below right: *Summer 2012, Brooklyn at Heffley Creek firing range near Kamloops. She is firing a .45 cal black powder rifle that belonged to my Grampa George Brown. Our family has always loved black powder shooting competitions. This was the first time I'd taken my kids to one. Prior to this, I had little interest in shooting any more firearms.*

Above left: *For Jacob's 7th birthday I took him dirt bike riding. He is deff Daddy's lil man. Loves the motorbikes.* Above right: *Jacob riding his quad in front of our house.* Below right: *Jacob at one of his hockey practices. He loves hockey. We've sat for years watching the games. His favorate players are Kipprusoff and Iginla and I am a die-hard Canucks fan. I blame his mom for dropping him on his head when he was a baby. No other way to explain the Flames being his favorite team :).*

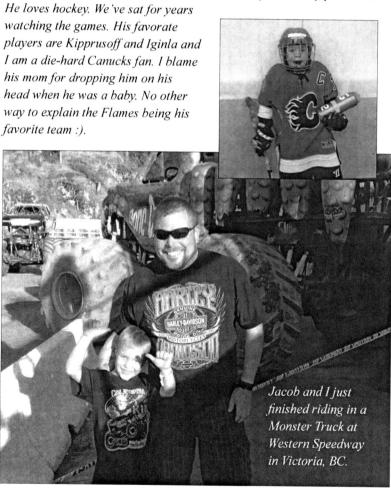

Jacob and I just finished riding in a Monster Truck at Western Speedway in Victoria, BC.

Left: *My little guy Jacob, age 8. We just came back from a ride on my friend's bike. Jacob was loving the side car.* Below: *Jacob and I at the races.*

Above: *Me sitting on an old Indian motorcycle that was at a store in a mall in Richmond. The owner was nice and let me sit on it. It would be a dream to own one.* Left: *Me at age 43. Taken at my cousin's wedding. I made the paddle as a gift for my cousin and his wife. This was the fifth paddle I had made. It is based on my favorite story,* Raven and the Light.

Above: *My girlfriend, Katherine, and me at our home, winter 2014.* Left: *My dad, Mike Brown, with Jacob, age 7. Photo taken at Heffley Creek, summer 2012.*

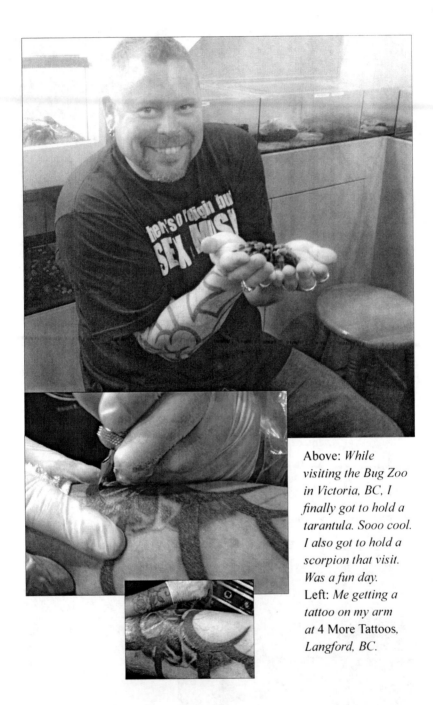

Above: *While visiting the Bug Zoo in Victoria, BC, I finally got to hold a tarantula. Sooo cool. I also got to hold a scorpion that visit. Was a fun day.*
Left: *Me getting a tattoo on my arm at* 4 More Tattoos, *Langford, BC.*

ABOUT THE POET

E d Brown was born in November of 1970 in Prince Rupert, BC to parents Michael James Stanley Brown and Daphne Lacroix. He lived in New Westminster, BC with his mother until the age of eight when he moved to Prince George, BC to live with his dad and step mom Heather. His summers were spent living in New Westminster with his mother.

While in Prince George he attended Wildwood Elementary and Kelly Road Secondary where he graduated. After high school Ed moved to Burns Lake, BC to work at Ray's OK Tire until he joined the Canadian Forces in October 1992.

Ed started his military career in Cornwallis, Nova Scotia where he attended basic training. Then it was off to Shilo, Manitoba where he attended Royal Canadian Horse Artillery battle school. Next, Ed was posted to 2 RCHA Canadian Forces Base Petawawa, Ontario, where he was assigned as a gunner in E Battery Delta Troop. Ed went on his first tour to the former Yugoslavia in 1993. While in Petawawa, Ed spent a year with the Special Service Pipes and Drums learning to play the bagpipes.

Ed changed his military trade in 1997 when he applied to go to the Navy as a Naval Combat Information Operator. Upon completion of his NCIOP training in Halifax, Nova Scotia, Ed was posted to CFB Esquimalt, Victoria, BC where he served on *HMCS Calgary, Regina, Winnipeg* and *Moresby*.

In 2000, due to frequent seasickness, Ed had a medical remuster to Mobile Support Equipment Operator, a position he held until releasing in December of 2011.

During his career Ed visited about twenty different countries, had three tours of duty, and wore Army, Navy and Air Force uniforms.

He now lives in Victoria, BC with his children Amanda, Brooklyn and Jacob. In his spare time he enjoys riding his Harley, playing goalie in floor hockey, helping assistant coach his son's minor hockey and learning First Nations Art.

Ed is currently working on a diploma in Water and Wastewater Technologies, training for his new career as an operator.

CPSIA information can be obtained at www.ICGtesting.com
Printed in the USA
LVOW13s1356300714

396405LV00008B/24/P